Self-care Kit to Mental Wellness

A Transformative Guide to Boosting Your Mental Health For Holistic Living

Queentah Wambulwa

Dear Danao, thank you
for your support. As you
go through this book,
hope you find inspiration
for your wellness.

Queentah
21/2/24

Printed and Bound by:

PUBLISH4ALL
Kenya

p4akenya@gmail.com
0798674454

Cover design by Cliff Mboya - Publish4All Kenya Ltd

First Edition: December 2020

ISBN: 978-9914-706-77-2

ACKNOWLEDGEMENTS

If my life had been full of bliss ever since I was born, no hitch on the way, this book would not have existed. I once heard someone say that suffering should never be in vain. It must birth something good, something helpful, not only to the person in question but to those around them. The creation and birth of this self-care kit emanates from such.

I am glad that my struggle with mental illness did not come empty-handed. I have met many people along the way, some of whom I believe I would not have come across if every bit of my life was perfect. I have learnt great lessons and become a different person all together. So I extend my deepest gratitude and thanks to everyone who has crossed my path to help me become the person I am today.

A special thank you goes to Dr. Linda Nyamute, the psychiatrist who never seems to tire when I bounce millions of questions her way. Your love and patience are ingredients much needed in this world. Live forever Doc!

Esther Ingolo and the team at the Situation Room, Tononoka, who fired my spirit and passion for fellow mankind. You are truly awesome!

The CAS in the Information and Communication Technology Ministry, Nadia Ahmed, together with Mahmood Noor, Edward Kute, Dr. Omondi, Corazon Aquino, Gates Mgenge, Stephanie

Maseki, Paul Akwabi, Muscat Moreno, Nuru Bahati, Dr.Raila Pius, Ruthalia Michael, Brian Emmanuel, Liz Ombati, Fathma Hajj and Michael Njenga who held my hand and gave me opportunities to speak about my mental health course. You are a unique circle of friends, I salute you all.

Great appreciation goes to the team at Amani Counselling Centre for imparting the knowledge I needed to understand myself and others. Your training in counselling psychology helped birth this book to an extent I cannot measure. Your generosity transformed me.

Clive Lupao, my homeboy who from 23 years and counting of knowing me still calls me friend. There is no one who can tell my story better than you. You have cheered me during my good times and encouraged me when I was falling apart. You are a special kind of hero.

To Musa Oyoo, my model manager, your humility and dedication to your job have landed me great opportunities and the expansion of my social network. Things you do for my organization, Girls for Girls Africa Mental Health Foundation (G4G Africa) will forever fire my heart. You inspire me to be a better person every day.

Professor Laila Abubakar, the Vice Chancellor of Technical University of Mombasa and the Editorial team led by Dr. Victor Lutsili, Serah Welime and the Dean of students, Dr. Joel Oluoch who ensured endless moral and emotional support when I needed it most. I appreciate your trust and the opportunity you afforded me to deliver the commencement speech during the 7th Graduation in 2019. Such an honourable opportunity, thank you.

Pastor Michael Mugera, Pastor Cornellius Karandini, Pastor Wilkister Wekesa and the entire Friends Church,Quakers who offered spiritual support. You made sure that all the spiritual wolves were kept at bay giving me a chance to rise up after every fall. You have shown me love beyond measure.

A huge thank you to my primary, high school and campus buddies who have not only kept in touch despite seasons and places; Derrick Karungani, Felix Muthui, Berrita Lusweti, Faith Wafula, Elvis Namusasi, Simon Kupalia, Elizabeth Ressa, Vivian Kisaka, Lynn Wayeta, Esther Oulo, Jael Janis, Cynthia Ambani, Matilda Nekesa, Cedrick Wandera, Sharon Lucy, Ezra Mulusa, Grace Unah, Dennis Okanga, Rose Bett, Edwin Talla , Lucy Nyikuri, Maureen Gikonyo, Faith Ngachi and Grace Kuvuna. Your dedication to true and strong friendship has made my life easier.

Twain Pictures, Touch by Laura, Style's Collection, Mikaye Restaurant and Alliance Française de Mombasa Director, Vincent Padare who made sure this self-care kit would have a face like no other. Wherever it goes, your fingerprints will go also. You all are a wonder.

My writing mentor and editor, Magdalene Kamau-Otieno, who directed me on structuring my story to help the millions who need to win in the game of mental wellness, thank you. We are winning in this!

To the wonderful individuals I have connected with online and met in various conferences, you know yourselves. I love you.

And finally, to my parents, Sir Dickens and Rael Wambulwa, your heroic efforts in helping me understand the value of family, true love and the emotional support you keep pouring into my life keeps me going. Because you believe in me, I have learnt to believe in myself. Thank you also for praying for me every single day. To my lovely brothers Joel, Calistus, Junior and Keith, you continually remind me that unconditional love comes first. To my grandparents, cousins and close friends, you stood by me when I needed you most. Thank you!

This self-care kit is dedicated to every person who has experienced the wrath of compromised mental health and is devoted to up their game to stay well and help others around them enjoy the rare pleasures of mental wellbeing. Stay strong and remember you are now in a better position to help others.

Content

Part 1

Demystifying Mental Health

Chapter 1

What is it?

What comes to your mind when you hear the term 'Mental health'?

You probably have heard it a gazillion times over the last three years, it almost feels like a buzzword. But if it were, it would have faded into the thin air by now. Three years is too long for any buzzword to survive. So it is not. And that is why you and I ought to lend it some space in our hearts right away.

So what really is mental health and why is it such a big deal around the world?

The two words in their simplest form create a picture of the ability to live life in its fullness. Meaning that you are flexible enough to handle life's challenges as they come by creating suitable solutions. That does not mean you are a version of Superman or Batgirl.

No.

It humbly means you are able to identify different situations, analyse and handle them as they come. Handling them includes seeking for help when necessary. This is a continuous process, so as long as you live your mental well-being must remain a concern.

Your mental health then determines how you think, feel, relate with people around you, make choices and cope with everyday life.

The World Health Organization (WHO) further adds that mental health also includes how you perceive your ability to succeed while pursuing a certain goal, your well-being in relation to what you believe, your self-governing ability, your ability to do something well and your ability to reach your full potential. It is a mouthful of expectations, yet these are just a few items in the basket.

So where there are mental health problems or compromised mental well-being, that is where mental illness begins.

However, a person can have satisfactory mental health and still be mentally ill and one who does not have any mental illness can be considered as having poor mental health. Only when there are diagnosable behavioural and mental patterns in a person's life can we point fingers at mental illness.

And that makes mental health such a wide field.

The basic definition above therefore allows you to identify when your mental health is compromised enabling you to take action. You then can turn to a friend or a family practitioner who is then able to direct you to places where you can get help. That is where psychologists, psychiatrist, therapists and social workers aid in administering the right kind of help.

That sounds good until you realize that in most developing countries the vibe on mental health is just beginning to take root. Meaning, a share of the population in most African countries may have their mental health compromised and still not know it.

Let us start right here in Kenya. Have you heard of the saying, 'Every market has a mad man'?

When you enquire why a mad man, some people say it is a sign that the market is productive. The deal is further sweetened by saying that for a person to be mad, they must have crossed someone else's path and had witchcraft shot their way. And the fellow is left to wander into the market. Or is it to enrich the market?

Madness is hardly seen as a mental health problem but as a scoop of spiritualism gone wrong; being possessed by a demon.

Whether this is true or not, I will let you digest. But by now I hope you realize how easy it is for a community to alienate one of their own just because the person in question seems under alien influence. How much more those who maintain their silence, never walk around naked or laden with bags of litter heading nowhere; they seem to have it all together from the outside?

I am talking of those friends who spell all their text messages well, keep them short as if always minding their own businesses and respond to your greetings with, 'I'm fine.' Could they be suffering from the inside but are afraid to say so lest they face alienation?

Do you now see why I am fussing about mental health and mental illness?

The fuss is inevitable because I now understand that compromised mental health manifests in more than the one way that seems all so familiar; running mad. And some of these cases tiptoe around unnoticed up until the victim descends into ceaseless gloom.

That is where this self-care kit comes in.

I have been down that road, all the way to the psychiatric centre at Kenyatta National Hospital in Nairobi, Kenya. Not as a psychiatrist, psychologist, or Yoga teacher, but as a patient.

Yes, you read that right. But before I tell you my story, let us play a game.

Pick the Brain

The idea here is to take a break off the kit, have a little fun as you confront your point of view on the subject of mental health.

Break Game: Shoot into the Bowl	
Requirements	An empty bowl, a timer and five balls made from pairs of socks.
Instructions	Place the empty bowl five meters away, set the timer to sixty seconds and try shooting the balls into the bowl one at a time while attempting each question below aloud. Do not empty the bowl until all the five balls are in and you have responded to the question at hand. Shooting the ball continues until the timer beeps. When the timer goes off, do not shoot any more balls if you still have any left. Instead, take a minute to note down the response you gave for the question at hand. Proceed to the next question only after fulfilling these instructions.

Question 1	Now that you know what mental health means in brief, how would you describe your mental wellness right now?
Question 2	Think of the last mad man or woman you saw and try to imagine their life before they got into that state. Their family, friends, belief system, the school they attended, favourite food or hangout joints. What do you think their earlier life looked like?

Question 3	How well are your friends, family and neighbours informed about mental health?

Chapter 2

Why Am I Bothered?

Campus life began on a high note. I first lived in a hostel like every other student. But not for long. By the second semester, I moved to a decent fully-furnished apartment in one of Mombasa's beautiful estates. It was not the kind of place an ordinary first year student would live in unless they originated from a very well-to-do family.

I am the first of the five children of my father. The only daughter, but even that does not warrant why I lived in a house my parents could not afford.

My father is neither a politician nor a business tycoon. He is your everyday high school teacher with a salary he occasionally needs to riot for to convince his employer that he is worthy of it. He is also a devout Christian. Oh and my mother, she is a community activist. Let us not discuss her salary for now.

So where on earth was this first year student getting the kind of money to live a life her own parents could only dream about?

No, I did not sell my kidney, but way back in February 2012, I fell helplessly in love with the son of a rich man from Lugulu in Bungoma County, my home village. I was in Form 2, a 16-year old student in a decent high school. He was 24, good looking and in charge of his family's property in Kenya. The weightier percent of his family members lived abroad.

I was a bright student scoring high in academics and rocking the world in extracurricular activities; drama, music and even as a girl guide. I threw my extroverted energies in everything that dared entice me. I dreamed of becoming a lawyer; quite a tall order for a girl who spent her holidays carrying jerry cans of water on her head from the river, making mud dolls and eating wild fruits!

But being gregarious comes with its own problems. You see, I love people, and when I love, I love with every atom of my being. So when it came to loving the son of a rich man, neither my parents' vehement protests nor my average background mattered. Call it naivety, but he was my love, my light, my all. And whatever he said became my law!

So when I completed high school in 2014, scored B Plus and got the invitation letter to pursue Bachelors of Commerce at Technical University of Mombasa, I took this as my one-way ticket to freedom.

My father could hear none of it. He was fed up with my reckless life and wanted me close home where he would groom me into a responsible woman. As a respected man in the village and the church, he understood that it was required of him to raise disciplined children. To be the man whose kids toed the line by default, a lifetime assignment he lived for.

But my boyfriend had passed the law; he was going to pay my school fees and upkeep. Of what use was my father's refusal?

I planned to leave home for Mombasa without my father's knowledge. I told my mother about it hoping she would keep the secret between us. Boy was I wrong. I should have known that her loyalty was always to him. The plan failed. So I came up with Plan B, to go further against him and report him to the church leaders so they would persuade, or maybe coerce him to allow me travel to Mombasa for my studies.

It worked!

That evening all emotions went high as the pastor and church elders visited my family persuading my father to let me go to the Mombasa campus. I alerted my boyfriend of the new development and he agreed to join me in Mombasa after my parents had cleared the school admission process.

I joined campus in September 2015 in the land of palm trees, sandy beaches and blue skies for the better part of the year; Mombasa *raha*. The coincidences of the first time fell into place; first time in Mombasa, first time being with my boyfriend with no parental supervision and first time living far away from home!

Add to that mix the luxurious apartment my boyfriend later rented for me, the reason why hostels were out of bound for this Bungoma girl. What else could a girl smitten by love ask for?

If there was a time I fell in love with being in love, this was it.

By the time classes began, the village in me had long departed and my sociable character was busy composing my clique with every classy born-town who could match my standards. After all, my rich boyfriend could get me anything I wanted anytime; bills, baggage and bonus to send home to my family. I was his, all his and totally dependent on him.

You could say I was a kept woman, but there is something pure about the first love that goes beyond the status of a partner. It is called LOVE, and I had it all and that kept our relationship firm.

Campus life was fun; I earned the title Boss Lady and to some, Slay Queen because my standards were piles above basic. Whether in the real world or the virtual plagued with social media, my following was large. My fame was towering. This went on throughout my first and second year.

I travelled to Nairobi often to see my boyfriend and when I returned, I came back to the lush apartment, my home. By this time marriage plans were underway, we would tie the knot immediately after my graduation. It was a done deal.

Then came the third year. I dropped in at my boyfriend's place unannounced just to find another lady in the same bed we had shared all along. The shock!

Why? What had I done to deserve the humiliation?

Worse still, he introduced me to her as his ex-girlfriend. It did not make sense to me, we had not disagreed prior to this visit, but here I was trying hard to defend my position to the same man I had given up my parents' love for. How was this possible? Had the distance taken him away from me?

I loved him. I knew all along that he had three children from three different ladies and had never let that deter my love for him nevertheless define him. I had loved him in spite of it all and was willing to fight for him. He was my man, all mine.

My life was shuttered. I had only one place to go, not to the posh apartment in Mombasa, but to my village, to the only person I knew would heal my wounds. My mother.

She advised me against making drastic decisions about the relationship. Besides, this is the same man I had no problem disrespecting my parents about. He had taken care of me in return, he had loved me just the way I desired it, and he had loaded my financial life with all the good things. Surely a little forgiveness would heal the misunderstanding.

I returned to Mombasa feeling betrayed, ashamed and guilty. Defeated is a better term with the hurt in my heart rising beyond threshold. I wanted him back. I needed him for many reasons but top in the list, I needed him so I could continue living the life I had been accustomed to. I was drunk with him, his love and the lovable girl he made me.

Lucky for me, he agreed to stand by me or be it until I came across another boyfriend who could take his place. It was convenient. It fit the bill just as I needed it even though I knew that I had lost a hugeous portion of him.

Little did I know that a massive slice of me had cracked. The love part. The part that demanded me to love myself in spite of my past failures. So to seal the cracks I sunk into drug use. Then most of the activities I engaged in at school became tasteless, all except my studies. I stopped caring for my social media fans and alienated myself from modelling which I was well known for. I even stopped hanging out with friends.

Food ceased making sense. I began losing weight and soon that glorious slay queen sparkle lost its lustre. Before I knew it, my whole clique was gone and smoking sat in their place. My whole world went foggy.

Then my cousin Eric saw me, we had not met in a long while. My state, deplorable. I was withdrawn, as if carrying the whole world on my shoulders. I narrated the whole saga, every detail of it. He could not bear seeing me this way. So he suggested that instead of rushing home from school now that I did not have my clique, the gym would fill the void much better.

Back to my boyfriend turned ex, I spoke to him about it, after all he had promised to support me financially until I found myself another man. He agreed to foot my gym subscription. I may have lost him, but I still had this part of him, the caring part that I needed.

The gym worked out wonders. It distracted me from overthinking, not from the drugs though. But this was much better. Good enough that I met a lovely man who like me was going through a tumultuous season, a story he shared with me. He was a divorcee with 2 kids to it. We became friends, real good friends that on one Friday he asked me out.

I was not ready for a new man in my life. I had school, a lifestyle to adjust and a man to let go. So I turned him down over and over until I felt ready for him.

The outing was great, an evening of indulgence or shall I say over indulgence that led to a sleepover and by now you know how that story goes. We had sex, unprotected!

Two weeks went by and life was getting better. The school, gym, home routine had reached perfection. I did not think about the unprotected intercourse episode much. It was just a by the way all until a friend I had met at the gym burst my bubble. I had asked her about him to which she warned me against sleeping with him. According to her, he was HIV positive!

Say what now?

We had long crossed that bridge and done it raw. Just when I thought I had found a man of my liking then this?

I did not work out that day; instead I went to a nearby hospital and did the Elisa Test. The results came back negative. No, I did not rejoice. In my mind, I was infected and maybe the virus had not manifested to a noticeable level.

'I must be HIV positive too. I know I am' became my personal anthem. I was slain, a walking dead.

Then I swung into the blame game accusing the man of infecting me with the deadly disease. Whether this made me feel better, I do not remember. He agreed to go for a test with me. Again the result came negative, but I did not believe him. So I indulged in self-diagnosis with Uncle Google as my right-hand man. And as you now he does not disappoint, he confirmed my worst nightmare. I had every sign and symptom depicting the presence of the virus in my system.

This led to yet another hospital visit, a test, another hospital visit, a test and on. The results came negative, negative and more negative. But my head could hear none of it. Not even the testing recommended after three months of the fateful event could settle me. The results read negative, but I believed I was positive.

Whether I was in denial, I do not know, but I was laden with renewed guilt, fear and hatred for food. I grew skinny, weak and felt sick round the clock. I just wanted to die!

And when death decided to delay, I opted for a shortcut. How about diving down the famous Nyali Bridge?

Not for a swim. No, for eternity.

Someone found me just before I parachuted down the mighty bridge and began rebuking me. I remember the harsh voices, many of them asking me why I wanted to commit suicide. They must have noticed my mortified system leaning frailly on the vertical rails as if calculating the distance and amount of energy needed to cover the feet below, head first.

They took me to Nyali Bridge Medical Centre, a hospital near the bridge for help. There I explained to the doctors that I was HIV positive and had no desire to pursue the remaining bits of my dreams. I wanted to be excused out of the world.

They listened, consulted and then carried out the test I had all grown accustomed to. Again, it turned out negative. But in my mind I was sure they had missed it, I was positive and like all other times, it broke me all over again.

Then the unfamiliar words oozed out of the doctor's mouth. The tests were right, but I was sick. Sick in a way that I did not know, in a way only a few people would understand. My mental health had been compromised in a big way. How and why I did not understand, but I needed help, so they said.

They suggested I see a friend of theirs at Kenyatta National Hospital. That is how I became a guest of the Psychiatric unit, Mental Health Section for one and a half months!

Pick the Brain

	Retrospective Activity
1	Are there parts of my life that resonate with the state of your life right now? *Be honest with yourself and note them down here.*
2.	Would you be willing to speak to someone you trust about them? *List at least three people you have confidence in and you can open up to about it.*

3.	What are your honest thoughts about checking in for psychiatric help and taking the prescribed medication?

Part 2

Understanding Where You Are

Chapter 3

Can You Spot the Difference?

When your mental health is compromised, you may not be in a position to identify it immediately. However, people around you may be able to see certain changes. It is unfortunate that some of those changes are easy to dismiss in their initial stages only for someone to say, "I thought I heard her say she was tired of living" when it is too late.

Chances are you have heard someone saying they are stressed, or even used this term yourself. Does that mean your mental health is compromised?

Well, it could mean that you are tired and in need of a well-deserved break. But it could also mean you are faced with a situation where you are not in a position to come up with the solution you need. And the situation in question keeps popping up in your life no matter how hard you try to solve or ignore it.

A good example is when you are cash trapped and your landlord decides to show up at your doorstep with a mighty padlock three times a day threatening to throw you out. Worse still, your borrowing quota is exhausted and none of your friends can bail you out.

Or when you are about to sit for your exams but cannot get a day or two off from work so you can polish up in your revision.

The two situations can be dismissed as 'normal life occurrences', but there is nothing normal about them when they linger a little longer in your mind. If your brain cannot find a way out of them, you may begin to feel antsy about them. And before you know it, they drag along other discomforts ranging from lack of sleep, to worry, fear and unexplained body aches.

The longer the situation at hand remains unsolved and becomes part of your every-minute thoughts, the more likely you are to show signs and symptoms that your physician diagnoses as mental illness.

By this time, the situation has invited other shortfalls. You are not only falling behind in rent but also disregarding work, ignoring all phone calls and avoiding friends. You further become an easy target to many other problems.

Does the saying, 'A problem always comes with its relatives' now sound sensible?

Signs of Mental Illness

Sometimes the situation at hand is not something other people can easily intervene in like the case of rental arrears or inability to access days off to prepare for an exam. It could be the loss of a loved one or when a lover decides to end the relationship for whatever reason like it was in my case.

As long as the situation and its relatives continue renting space in your daily thoughts in a way to indicate defeat, your mental health becomes compromised. Remember, it is human nature to emerge the winner in the toughest difficulties. That is why we celebrate when we solve even the least of the snags in our lives. When we see the light at the end of the tunnel.

But when you cannot find the victorious end of a situation, different versions of helplessness hijack your thoughts.

You may begin feeling angry when someone brings up the topic you feel defeated to solve. You become unfriendly to the person because you feel they are 'in our case'. Sometimes you may even opt to get physical with them.

You may also want nothing to do with people who you are familiar with, your drive for things you once found pleasure in may come to a halt for no comprehensible reason and somehow you want 'space'.

I remember feeling this way; though I was a well-known model at school, I stopped showing up for modelling sessions and stopped updating my social media community on what I was up to. I felt miserable, detached and was always worrying about what people thought about my new ex-slay queen status. Most of all, I worried about my HIV status even after testing negative for every test I did.

I also withdrew from friends while others just took off, multiplying the loneliness. Eating became a difficult task and in its place came substance abuse. With nothing in life to look forward to, I began contemplating suicide.

But you do not have to feel as I did for a physician to declare a state of mental illness. You could however show symptoms such as depleted sleep, unexplained tiredness, mood swings, hallucinating and excess feeling of fear.

There may also be changes in sexual drive and this can swing either way; a strange crave for it or complete unwillingness to venture into that world. This may also happen with appetite for food and alcohol. Understanding people around you may turn out difficult and concentrating on activities you need to becomes compromised. Sometimes the state of confusion may also step into the mix.

In my case, the inability to cope with the rejection followed by the fear of being HIV positive left me feeling unwanted, unworthy of love and undeserving of life. It persuaded me to end my life.

It is important to note that some people do not bring up suicide in their daily conversations. That does not mean they do not contemplate it. Other people do. And then there are those who never consider it at all.

Some Types of Mental Illness

While the doctor diagnosed my case as depression and anxiety, there are many other mental illnesses today. The most common include anxiety disorders, depression disorders, post-traumatic stress disorder (PTSD), schizophrenic disorders, and bipolar disorders.

Since this is a self-care kit, I will not go into deep details regarding these illnesses. Instead, I will focus on the two I experienced in brief and then share the different areas I focus on to ensure mental wellness. The good news is that you can use the kit to nurture your mental wellness with this content.

Anxiety Disorder

This happens when a person displays prolonged seasons of worry about certain things. Such can range from their health, routines, and interactions with other people. Your physician is likely to term such as Generalized Anxiety Disorder.

It makes you irritable, tense, unable to control worry or fear, feel tired, restless, edgy and tampers with your sleeping pattern such that you feel deprived of sleep. I had each one of these symptoms when I believed I was HIV positive.

Anxiety can also present itself as panic disorder delivering sudden seasons of intense fear peaking in a matter of minutes or phobia-related disorder, where you are terrified of certain situations.

However, Generalized Anxiety Disorder is the most common type of anxiety and it sometimes goes unnoticed despite showing up most days within half a year period.

Depression Disorder

Symptoms of depressions tend to occupy the better part of the day, every day for not less than two weeks. You could experience pains in your head, stomach alongside digestive difficulties, drastic changes in appetite and weight, extreme sadness, emptiness, guilt, helplessness, low confidence and energy leading to sluggish walking or speech.

You may also have problems concentrating, remembering and keeping still, change in your sleeping pattern, reduced interest in hobbies and work as well as suicidal thoughts or attempts.

There are various forms of depression such as postpartum depression that is experienced by women after delivery. This is a case where the woman experiences extreme tiredness, anxiety and sadness. Some women feel disconnected from the baby and may not want to take care of them.

Then there is persistent depression where some of the symptoms mentioned here last for about two years. In psychotic depression, the person has disturbing false but fixed beliefs. They may claim to hear or see things. And Seasonal Affective Disorder (SAD) tends to show up during specific seasons where the affected person experiences the symptoms of depression. As soon as the season is over, they resume to their original self.

Judging from my story in Chapter 2, it should be now easy for you to understand why the physician from Nyali Bridge Medical Centre gave the depression and anxiety diagnosis. Before venturing in what causes mental health disorders such as I went through, a game of self-evaluation is in order.

It is play time!

Pick the Brain

This game helps you evaluate how you feel and see if there is a good reason why.

The Game of How and Why?	
Look back into the last two weeks, how would you describe how you have been feeling most of the time? *Happy, Sad, Excited, Anxious, Okay, Tired, Rested, Other.*	Give further details:
Does how you have been feeling affect your relationship with people around you?	Explain how?

How would you define your sleeping pattern in the last two weeks? *Is there any notable change, and if so, is it justifiable?*	Evaluate.
How about your ability to concentrate on matters that require your focused attention? *Evaluate your ability to concentrate and remember the details of the activities you engage in.*	How would you rate such?
Is there a healthy balance between various parts of your life; your you-time, work, family and friends? *Watch out for guilty feelings when the balance is affected.*	Explain.

Chapter 4

What Causes Mental Illness?

There have been quite a number of guesses as to what causes mental illnesses. And with the, 'It runs down a family' popping up in various discussions, genetics becomes the most obvious reason.

However, progressive research points to a party of three; biological, environmental and psychological reasons.

Though genetics seem to take the larger share of the blame as far as the biological factors are concerned, there are many other culprits. They include physical accidents leading to brain injury, interference in the brain development of an unborn child, trauma during birth, long-term substance abuse, poor nutrition and exposure to toxins in air, water and food consumed. These should never be overlooked as they hinder normal operation of the brain cells.

As for the environmental factors, they may not directly cause the problem but they are aggravators encouraging the state of mental illness in a person who is already vulnerable. The factors to watch out for include drug abuse by the person or someone they are close to, broken family, divorce or death of a parent, social expectations, inability to cope with changes at school, work or family and low self-esteem.

The most common psychological factors include rejection, inability to relate with other people well and trauma caused by physical, sexual and emotional abuse.

These are a few of the known factors and only when certain signs and symptoms show up is the person diagnosed as having mental illness. The good news is that you do not have to wait for the suicidal thoughts to pop up in your mind to take action as it was in my case.

What Caused Depression and Anxiety in My Case

Sustaining your mental health is a lifetime journey. And if it has at one time been compromised, it can turn out long. But the length of this journey should not worry you; your concern should be the Johnny Walker famous slogan, 'Keep Walking'.

Why?

Because it is possible to sink back into the type of mental illness you have been through before with every hit that you experience every day. This fact did not register in my mind until it started happening.

The first hit came about when I found my boyfriend with another lady and he declared me his ex-girlfriend in her presence. I was angry at first, then hurt. The thought of being without him destroyed me, and then a series of 'why' set in as I wondered where I had gone wrong.

But I needed to return to school and function well. So, I began using drugs as a coping mechanism; something to knock off the misery. They seemed to cover for the hollowness in my heart. But there was one huge problem; every time the drugs wore out, I was empty all over again and it was time for a refill.

A mix of working out at the gym and drugs for a while seemed to do the trick until I was told that the man I had slept with without protection was HIV positive. With every test turning negative, a voice inside me screamed otherwise. The second hit.

I thought I had broken every last nerve in me, but the repeated 'negative' news broke me even further. If that is even possible. I shoved myself into a dark space. So while those who rescued me from the suicide attempt thought they were saving me, my spirit had long died, my body was only trying to follow its leader.

Only after the doctor's explanation did I understand that I had suffered depression and anxiety.

My inability to answer the 'whys', failure to forgive myself for not heeding my parents' advice and the fear of being HIV Positive or the denial thereof came in as one package. But with the drugs as an aggravating factor, my chances of recovering on my own were slim.

This, I would not have figured out on my own. I needed help to see the illness for what it was. And so does everyone suffering from mental illness.

The Ups And Downs

While at the psychiatry centre I realized that part of recovery involved speaking out. I was encouraged to tell my story so that I did not harbour any bitterness against those who hurt me or myself.

Soon I was on my way to recovery and was grateful to be alive, again. I made up my mind to begin a foundation, Girls for Girls Africa Mental Health Foundation (G4G Africa) as a sign of gratitude for mental wellness.

My aim was and still is to use the foundation as a vehicle to reach out to girls and women in every community I find myself in on matters concerning mental health. This would create a safe space for them to share their dreams and disappointments, find their own identity and rise above any self-esteem issues cropping up.

I understood that not everyone would be in a position to access the kind of facilities and the help I was receiving. Again, through the organization, those sinking into depression would have early intervention so they did not have to go through the mess I had put myself into; drugs, self-neglect and attempted suicide. Or any kind of self-harm for that matter.

When I left the hospital, I returned to school and life seemed quite alright. I challenged myself to vie for the students' president position using my story as part of my manifestos. I knew that there were many students who were going through emotional turmoil but hardly spoke about it. So I started 'Coffee with Queentah' hangout to allow students to open up about things they were going through.

It worked wonders!

My confidence in the recovery journey shot up when I realized that though I lost in the presidential bid, I remained strong. I continued with the mental health advocacy, empowering everyone I came across.

Soon I landed a great opportunity for industrial attachment with a huge organization pushing my confidence levels to the top. This came along with renewed confident to date all over again.

Being in love felt great, but the joy was short-lived as it tugged along the revelation that I could not have this man to myself. He was married. Such heartbreak!

For the next one month I sunk into depression again. The third hit!

Whether bad luck in matters concerning love or the forces of nature working against me, I did not understand. All I know is that it hurt, badly.

This time round though, I had learned the art of speaking out and was still attending therapy sessions. So I chose to be fair to myself and the man. I forgave both of us leading to quicker recovery

The fourth hit came after the story about my journey into depression featured in the Daily Nation newspaper on October 18, 2018. My school had requested me to share my story with the first-year students which led to numerous interviews with local media and extreme publicity. The gospel of mental health was flying in every direction I could ever dream of.

But this came with its own agony as the very next day nude photos and videos of me and a female friend portraying us as lesbians were leaked on social media, sent to the school and worst of all to my family!

Not only did this harm the image I had been rebuilding but it also hurt my parents. They had been so kind to me and had stood with me throughout the recovery period. But this blow tarnished their standing in the community. No one could have prepared them for the cyberbullying as it tore through their hearts and mine.

Worse still, visiting home became torturous as *boda boda* riders hurled ugly names my way whenever they saw me. Anyone among them who did not know the story of the nudes was quickly updated making the situation even worse.

But the shame did not end there. When I went to my home church I found out that they too knew the story of the nudes and the cyberbullying. No matter how much I tried to contain the situation, it was obvious I had brought shame to the entire village. Would I ever be able to show my face at home again?

Every time I look back into the four hits, I remind myself that every hit had its purpose in the conception of this self-care kit. It would have been worse if after all the ups and downs nothing was birthed. But something was; a strong woman born to strengthen others.

It is your turn now to get strong!

Pick the Brain

The idea here is to take a break off the kit, and practice the art of bouncing back after every hard hit.

Break Game: Bounce Back	
Requirements	A tight ball made from pairs of socks stuffed into one, a timer, a wall you can toss the ball onto and a chair to sit in. Set the timer to sixty seconds then keep throwing the ball against the wall and try catching it while sitting in your chair. In between the throws and catches, try to answer the questions below. Each question should take only one minute to answer and a minimum of thirty throws and catches. Remember to aim at the highest point of the wall each time you throw. This should be fun! Take an extra minute to record the answer to each question here.

Question 1. Remember the last time someone hurt you badly. If someone else hurt you in the same way a little later, how would you handle yourself and them?	
Question 2. How long do you allow painful and angry thoughts to linger in your mind after the incident causing such takes place and why? *Use the last three incidents you remember to evaluate.*	

Part 3

Making Self-care Personal

Chapter 5

Do You Want to be Free?

Have you heard the warning, 'Do not wait to lose something to acknowledge its value'?

The one thing I longed for most while I was hospitalized was my happy, vibrant and guilt-free self. That was girl I had been before the dark heavy cloud of anxiety and depression engulfed my life. The girl who left Lugulu in Western Kenya for the coastal city in pursuit of higher education and the promise of a brighter life ahead. The girl who loved campus life and all the goodies that came wrapped with it; modelling, an enviable social media following and the slay queen status!

Where had she disappeared to, when and why?

It had never occurred to me that I would one day wake up without her. I believed that version of me would always be there for me with or without making effort to take care of it.

But for the one and a half month I was at the hospital, as I regained my mental wellbeing, the value of that vivacious girl became real. I did not ever want to be unwell, sad, and dull, or burdened with guilt as I had before.

For one month I was under medication and what many call 'solution-oriented form of talk therapy' or Cognitive Behavioural

Therapy (CBT). Through the CBT sessions I learned a different way of thinking, acting and reacting to situations that had compromised my mental wellbeing.

I was encouraged to confront regular issues practically and challenge the beliefs I had adopted and were causing emotional turmoil instead of bottling them in my heart. Think of it as confronting your personal narrative; the story you tell yourself as true.

While this helped me regain my vibrant self, I realized I needed to devise a way to maintain this status for good!

That is when I came up with G4G Africa which would later inspire 'Coffee with Queentah' hangout. I wanted to make sure that no one around me would ever have to bottle up issues into depression or anxiety, at least not if I had a say about it. I would ensure they had a safe space to address the issues and be free.

Through the knowledge I gathered while undergoing CBT, engaging in Yoga classes and the counselling psychology studies I undertook in July 2020, I developed this self-care kit as my personal guide.

The self-care kit features eight areas of every human's life that when well nurtured assures all-round wellness; body, mind and spirit. It prepares you to walk through areas of your life that would otherwise threaten your wellbeing without cowering or throwing your hands up in defeat.

Remember, when one portion of your tripartite being; body, mind and spirit, is hit, the whole of you suffer. That is why I want you to have this kit.

Does that mean you will not bump into hurtful circumstances?

Does that mean you will have a tear-free life?

Does the self-care kit promise that your behind will not get whipped to the ground by different life circumstances?

No. No. And No.

But every time it happens, you will bounce right back up!

Better still, you will feel some of those circumstances coming and raise your gut-level in readiness.

Your story may not include hospitalization, but the need to live the true version of your life and grow in your desired endeavours cannot be overlooked. With this kit you will practically learn how to keep your mental health in check now that you have a clear picture of how the mental illness side of life feels through my story.

If you have been medicated before, this section will help you not revert into mental illness. It helped me rise from the filthiness of cyberbullying, a second heartbreak, humiliation by *boda boda* riders and the uneasiness I experienced when I visited my parents back home.

So instead of bowing to ‘once bitten twice shy’, my new narrative is, ‘once bitten now stronger!’ You too can change your narrative.

Are you ready?

Pick Your Brain

Guarantee Your Mental Wellbeing by Observing These Eight Areas		
1.	Physical Body Are you happy about your physical wellbeing at the moment? Explain.	
2.	Daily Nutrition Are you deliberate about what you eat for the sake of your mental health? Explain.	
3.	Spiritual wellbeing Are you at peace with who you are right now? Explain.	

4.	Emotional Wellness How do you summon your feelings into balance when tough times come your way? Explain.	
5.	Financial Wellness Are you in control of your money or money is controlling you? Explain.	
6.	Intellectual Wellness What new nuggets have you learned and applied in the last two weeks to better your life? Explain.	

7.	Social Wellness How are you pouring yourself into the lives of people around for their benefit? Explain.	
8.	Environmental Wellbeing How does your surrounding affect your mental health? Do you think you have control over it? Explain.	

Chapter 6

Is Your Body Ready?

When your mental health is compromised, it is your physical body that takes the beating. Let me explain the math here.

When you no longer want to eat, it is your body that loses weight. When you are depressed and only want to eat junk, it is your body that ends up ill, overweight or weary. When your sleeping pattern goes amiss, it is your body that suffers lethargy. When depression discourages you from paying attention to your hygiene, it is your body that looks and smells badly. And when your brain cannot figure out solutions to various problems and you seek comfort in drugs, it is your body that has to endure craves, aches and hangovers.

The list is endless.

Do you now see the connection?

Maybe I should remind you how I tortured my own body when I could not eat, sought the companion of cigarettes and even considered ending my life. Oh wait, that means killing my own body!

Now imagine reversing the whole reaction by taking care of your physical body so as to guarantee your mental wellbeing. Would that make sense?

Here are several ways to do just that.

Physical Exercise for Mental Wellbeing

Wendy Suzuki, an American neuroscientist, after conducting the effect of physical exercises on the brain concluded, "Exercise is the most transformative thing that you can do for your body today."

Exercising is not limited to going to the gym, even though that is worth investing in. You can start by engaging in rigorous activities at home such as thorough cleaning your home for at least two hours once a week. That translates to intense body movement.

Then you can graduate to taking early morning brisk walks around your estate in the name of catching the first ray of the sun or sunset chasing at a park near you.

You can also engage in aerobics, swimming, cycling, running or dancing as part of your physical workout.

While we are in this neighbourhood, let me bring to your attention the expressive therapy. It involves using art, music and other creative activities to help you manage your emotions and memories. This is where dancing comes in. Luck being on your side, today you can learn various ways of dancing from experts on YouTube and convert your sitting room to a dance floor.

Learn various dance moves from around the world with Matt Steffanina, keep it African and groove with Kukuwa Fitness or simply learn the Kenyan Odi Dance!

Expressive therapy also includes stage acting and demonstrative telling of the story of your life using imaginary characters.

Another great practice you could indulge in is Yoga. This is a group of physical and mental exercises whose origin is ancient India. While the spiritual aspect of Yoga is associated with Buddhism, Jainism and Hinduism, it is the meditation bit that captivates and then sets you free. We will visit the spiritual aspect in chapter 8.

Yoga includes sets of physical postures and breathing techniques that are vital in easing anxiety, weakening depressive symptoms and calming post-traumatic stress disorder. People who practice Yoga often are also able to quit smoking, reduce body weight, better cope with chronic diseases, improve on quality of sleep and have balanced emotional health.

Whatever physical exercise you choose, make sure it gets your heart thumping out of its comfort zone. Then you are guaranteed of immediate surge in good mood, increased attention span and bursting energy. This can sustain you for the better part of your active day.

But if you are looking for long-lasting results, which you should, research indicates that you engage in physical exercises for up to thirty minutes four days a week while aiming at increasing your heartbeat rate. Then you can expect the three benefits above plus increase in reaction time; quicker response to stimuli for your own good. You also guarantee your body a huge delay in the occurrence of any predisposed neurodegenerative disease such as dementia.

If this far you are not sold to working out on a daily basis because in the past there were no tangible results; the flat tummy, lean arms and strong legs you may have desired, now you have a new goal to watch out for. The secret is keeping your eye on the immediate mental benefit as well as the pension many years down your life.

Adequate Resting for Mental Wellness

While working out comes with its own bag of goodies, so does resting. It is unfortunate that many people today associate resting and sleeping with laziness or wasting time. Some even feel guilty about such. That explains the glorified boast, 'Who needs more than four hours of sleep daily?'

In fact, a common search on Google about sleep shows that many people want the same amount of rest they get from eight hours of sleep from only four hours.

Would you then blame your body for feeling fatigued all day, performing at half the capacity or dozing off in the middle of important activities?

It is unfair to ask from your body what you are not willing to deposit into it. So instead of waiting for anxiety to snatch away your sleep, practice giving your body enough rest. This includes six to eight hours of sleep, taking short relaxing breaks between tiring activities and listening to calming music especially before going to bed.

The best quality of sleep involves going to bed at a set time and deliberately sleeping for a set number of hours such that your wake up time is stipulated.

If you find it difficult to fall asleep immediately, try turning on some calming music one hour before going to bed; instrumental jazz works for most people. Consider selecting the kind of music that soothes your mind. This however is not a license to scroll through your mobile phone for YouTube or Social media indulgence. You will end up delaying the sleep or inducing irregular rest.

Oh, and there is no sin against taking an afternoon nap. You will be glad you did it!

The aim of sleep and relaxation breaks is to give your brain rest. The fewer the worries you drag into your rest, the better the quality. Then when you wake up, you will be ready to face the world.

Pick Your Brain

Ready Your Physical Body For Mental Wellness	
Requirement	Activities
Improving your quality of sleep *Which one of these activities do you need to work on from this point onwards?*	1. I only go to bed after completing all of my day's work, regardless of the time. 2. I wake up at a specific time every day. 3. I take my mobile phone to bed and scroll through until I fall asleep. 4. I drag the day's problem to bed so I can try to solve them there. 5. I think sleeping is for the lazy and weak.
Quality relaxation *Describe how you spend your relaxation moment in the space across.*	During my relaxation breaks, I ...

Exercising your body	For physical exercises, I will ...
Indicate in the box across the type of physical exercises you find exciting, are willing to engage in and how often, for your mental wellbeing.	

Chapter 7

What Did You Eat Today?

...and while answering that question, dare to take the phrase 'You are what you eat' literally.

When you make what you eat deliberate instead of a by-the-way, you protect both your physical body and your brain; the main culprit as far as your mental health is concerned.

There are two reasons why what you eat should concern you. The first is the fact that you are 100% responsible for what you put into your mouth. And second, the food that favours your heart in the long run favours your brain immediately and later in your life.

Meaning, if you eat what is right for the heart and the brain, you increase your chances of living an active, creative and memorable life. All of which you can do.

So what should you eat?

Your brain is such a demanding organ consuming a fifth of all the energy produced in your body. And since that energy emanates from the food you eat, eating for the sake of your brain is the most practical thing to do. So the direct answer to the above question would be, eat brain-worthy food.

This is a secret I wish I learned before I moved to Mombasa. Migrating from Western Kenya to the Coast meant a huge change in what I ate, the wild fruits and vegetables included. Let me explain why.

Top in the list of brain-worthy foods are the monounsaturated and polyunsaturated fats.

The monounsaturated fats are oils that remain liquid at room temperature but when chilled in your fridge, they turn solid. But for now, let us put the complex Chemistry aside. You can get these good fats from macadamia, cashew nuts, peanuts, olive oil and walnuts. Walnuts in particular contain a type of omega-3 fatty acid needed by the brain in large amounts.

The nut family promises to keep your brain's health in check. You only need to eat about 30 grams of your nuts of choice daily to meet your dietary requirements while lowering bad cholesterol and increasing the good type in your blood.

Oh, and just so you know, the good old avocado is a perfect source of monounsaturated fat too!

Polyunsaturated fats boast of being the king source of omega-3 and omega-6 fatty acid that you may have heard mentioned as key components in pills meant for increasing your brain power. Since your bodies have no ability to manufacture such, consider eating fish such as sardines, mackerel, trout and salmon. Otherwise turn to sunflower seeds and flax in low amounts.

The second group of brain-worthy foods is those containing antioxidants. They kick out oxidative stress from your system ensuring brain clarity, enhanced memory and slowed aging.

Antioxidants also delay the onset of neurodegenerative diseases in your system. This calls for falling in love with all those colorful vegetables and fruits you see in the market. Think of carrots, spinach, tomatoes, broccoli and the so-called wild vegetables. Consider also picking blackberries, blueberries and raspberries.

For starch, cut down on any processed foods. Most contain high fructose corn syrup (HFCS) that works against your brain's health. So if you must eat bread, eat the whole grain type. You may also want to befriend the *posho* mills for your cassava, maize, sorghum, millet and oats flour. Brown rice also works in your favour here.

Then there is a call to cut down on pre-salted meats such as found in salami, burgers and bacon. They are tasty yes, but the nitrogen in the meat and salt leave you dehydrated. And since the trend while eating such foods includes adding dressing sauces that contain HFCS and drowning the meal with soda, your body is exposed to unexplained thirsty and tiredness.

There is also a call to stay in touch with fresh milk, eggs, chicken and beef but in regulated intakes and careful preparation right in your kitchen. Note, the closer you are to the farm-fetched foods instead of fast foods, the better.

Finally in the name of consuming brain-worthy foods, make drinking water a daily and deliberate habit. Not only does water knock out thirst after eating foods with pre-salted meats or HFCS, but it also refreshes your body cells keeping them active.

You could start by filling two 1-litre bottles with clean water and placing them in places you frequent most as hydration reminders. Then sip the water at least twice every hour until they are both empty.

Good addiction if you ask me!

While our bodies are different, the foods recommended above when eaten with moderation and incorporated with physical exercises ensure adequate energy, practicable weight and great nutrition for your brain.

Help your brain help you. That power is your hands.

Pick your Brain

Deliberate Eating	
What kind of foods do you need to include in your weekly meal plan that you did not previously pay attention to?	
What kind of foods do you need to cut down to a bare minimum?	

Create your personal hydration trick. *It should include fresh water intake and fresh juicy fruits within your reach in their whole form.*	

Chapter 8

Are You at Peace with You?

While the issue of spirituality is seen as complex, I see it as a way of fostering a sense of inner peace and harmony in every part of your life. This brings clarity on why you are alive so you are connected with your purpose.

It also enables you to forge great and lasting relationships with people around you.

Spirituality in relation to your mental health enables you to become more patient when you cannot figure out difficult matters. It enables you to allow such to unfold at their own time instead of dwelling on why they are happening, to you. You are also able to appreciate the easier times instead of letting them pass unnoticed or in fear that they will fade away fast and leave you exposed.

The most common spiritual self-care practice around the world today is prayer. It involves staying connected with a higher authority you believe in. This does not necessarily mean being religious but being aware that you do not have to carry the day's difficulties alone. You have a place to seek refuge and a source of help in times of trouble.

Then there is meditation. To some people prayer is a form of meditation. To others, meditation is practiced as quiet reflection aimed at training your attention and awareness to achieve mental clarity, calmness and a stable state.

Meditation is also practiced through paying attention to incidences happening in the moment while purposefully being non-judgmental about them. That is mindfulness meditation.

It helps you not to dwell on stressful thoughts so that your brain is attentive and goal-focused. The opposite may include mind-wandering and daydreaming which could turn a good day unproductive.

Spirituality also enables you to craft personal standards, contribute to other people's wellbeing, show respect for other people's spiritual practices and be in communion with those of similar spiritual beliefs.

Regardless of the way you practice spirituality, ensure to release thoughts that destroy your inner peace and harmony hence compromising your mental health.

Pick Your Brain

Bettering Your Spirituality	
What activities do you engage in for your spirituality and how do they contribute to having peace of mind?	
State your top five values that you believe describe who you are and explain how they have helped you have inner peace.	

As a way of clearing your mind as you end this chapter, journal your thoughts for today. Then carry on journaling from this point on in a special diary.	
To end the exercise, spend the next 10 minutes in quietness or prayer for yourself without letting your mind wander into unproductive thoughts.	

Chapter 9

Can You Feel the Balance?

Life has an uncanny way of turning the world below your feet wobbly when you least expect it.

Just when you think the bliss from a morning walk will last the whole day, a knock at the door sweeps in disturbing news. As if that is not enough, the media alerts you of a fast spreading virus threatening to shut down the whole world in a second.

Not only is your personal life in turbulence, but also the world around you. And the ripples seem to widen fast, throwing you off balance!

So how in such conditions do you summon your feelings into a quick meeting to restore your emotional balance?

In comes emotional wellness.

This is the call to identify your immediate feelings, analyse them and decide the best way to handle them. It could mean working on them in person, delegating by reaching out to someone for support or simply watching them go by into the incinerator of your mind.

But sometimes we bottle up these feelings because we are ashamed, bitter or even believe how we feel is none of the other person's business.

The result, we keep regurgitating the feelings at hand until we are saturated with them. Then what was an emotional rollercoaster that would have been managed with the help of others solidifies into a mountain of anxiety throwing us into a series of 'what ifs' and 'but whys'.

We begin to question our every move preventing us from seeing the current moment for what it is.

Other times we sink into the valley of depression with regret or guilt wishing we had done things differently. We get so stuck in the past that we cannot move forward.

Regardless of how high on the mountain or deep in the valley you are, there is always a way out as long as you are breathing. That is where the phrase, 'no man is an island' comes in; the fact that you belong in a community.

So where do you begin?

Speak It Out

Not after the mental illness has struck, but way before that. It is the way your ancestors lived. They shared their thoughts and feelings with people around them. They acknowledged family, friends, wise ones and seers. They understood the power of 'a problem shared is a problem half solved'. They also shared their joys.

This too should be your way. Identify people who you can trust and are good listeners around you and create a workable relationship with them. Not because they will help you process every type of feeling that hits your life, but because they will listen.

Throughout the CBT sessions and my psychology classes, I noticed that therapists spent more time listening than giving advice. They would also ask questions to help me to open up a little more, examine a situation and then paint the picture of my life with the anger, excitement, shame and guilt I felt in colourful words. And every time I did it, the answer, peace and stability I sought popped up in my own words.

It worked like magic!

Forgive All

You have heard the saying, 'forgive, not so the other person may scot free, but so you may be free.' This is not just a nice concept, it is great practice.

While reaching out for help enabled me to understand the feelings bubbling from within, I found out that as I digested those feelings over the asked questions with a pinch of forgiveness I gained control. Then I was able to manage the emotional rollercoaster.

If you have ever been harmed by a person whom you believed was supposed to shield you from harm, forgiving them may not have come as the first topic you wanted to discuss with anyone.

But this is how I liken forgiveness.

Picture the person who harmed you carrying a heavy bag of ugly deeds and oozing more of such around you. Though they may have knowingly smeared you with the ugliness and spilled such around you making your ground slippery, whether to pick that heavy bag and carry it around is a personal decision.

If you do, you will find the process of leaving the mess they have created difficult because you carry the heavy bag in your hands and are left with nothing to reach out to others.

But if somewhere on the way you drop the heavy bag, you become light enough to grab the hand of the friend you are seeking help from.

Taking the heavy bag signifies taking offense. Whether the offense is thrust on you or you pick it in the process of the harm caused, keeping it compromises your emotional wellness. And before you know it your mental health will be at stake.

Again, most offenders rarely believe they are at fault. They may even justify their act by claiming that you asked for the harm they caused you. So they walk around guilt-free while you walk around offended.

You then become bitter and cannot stand meeting them, leave alone seeing them prosper. You are compelled to change routes, sit elsewhere during meetings where they are present and put a dash when you mean to mention their name. You are the burdened one. And they are free.

Forgiving them even when they do not deserve it means you refuse to hold that grudge in your heart and rent them space in your thoughts. This means setting yourself free.

But the juice does not end there. Forgiveness comes along with a good friend called self-acceptance. Think of it as inward love.

Accept Thyself

Throughout the season when I did numerous HIV tests, one thing stood out; doubt.

I refused to trust any other results other than what I had set my mind to believe. And then instead of keeping my mind open so I could manage the assumed condition, I clung on to the hurt.

However, when I began opening up during therapy sessions, the bottled up guilt, anger, shame and doubt began to ease. This created space for me to appreciate my life.

And though the new life did not match the seemingly perfect love-filled life I was accustomed to, it was a good enough platform for me to begin working upwards from.

It took forgiving myself for asking to be any different at that particular time and accepting that 'I am enough just as I am' for my emotions to calm into balance.

Does that mean I do not push myself to live better, have better and be better?

Absolutely not!

I want to be better so I can help others to do the same. But without accepting my current status and loving me for me, I would be out of balance. Therefore I would not make the positive impact I desire; this self-care kit, the hangouts and the foundation to mention but a few.

Pick Your Brain

Nursing You Into Emotional Wellbeing	
Review the week that was and pick out incidences that threw you out of balance in your emotions. *List the first five that come to mind.*	
How did you handle each one of them?	

Would you say you are now in control in each of the cases? *No anger, bitterness, guilt or shame such that you feel the need to act differently than you would on a regular day.*	
Go deeper and evaluate yourself for any past issue where you held back forgiveness of others and self or self-acceptance. *How does that affect your everyday life?*	

Chapter 10

Where is Your Money at?

Financial issues are among the top stressors in the world today. No matter where you turn, you are bound to bump into a person lamenting about the rising cost of living, inadequate cash flow or stubborn bills to mention but a few. Money never seems to be enough!

Now look back and recall the common narrative told to young scholars. Go to school, get a job and you will earn a lot of money and live a comfortable life. While the narrative may have favoured many in your community, someone in the same mix still complains about the inadequacy of money. They lack sleep over it. They disagree with others over it. Some even act uncouth just to get money.

If the rich, the mid and the poor are complaining about money, who then can solve the money problem?

You! Only you can solve your money problem.

It all begins with understanding how much of it you own, how much you have access to without harming yourself and others, and how far you are willing to venture to gather more while observing the legal and moral boundaries.

That is a mouthful, but that is what you need to manage your finances.

Let me break it down using some valuable lessons I learned during my recovery.

How Much Money Do You Own?

It takes humility to accept how much money you own. If you are employed or running a business, the figure is well known to you or can be approximated. That figure dictates the financial decisions you can make and actualize. That is where the statement, living within your means comes in.

It would be awkward to try acquiring things the money you earn cannot pay for. So do the math first to see how much you can spend without landing into debts or other life's nastiness. Otherwise, the same goodies you buy will come back to bite you!

This is one part of the financial wellness formula that I did not understand while growing up.

If you are unemployed and do not run a business, chances are you are under someone else's support. This means your budget is limited to what they can give you without being coerced. So before you make any financial decision, you must first seek their permission. As an adult, that may feel too humbling to bear, but it is the right thing to do. It helps you forge a way to earn your own cash.

How much money can you access without harming yourself and others?

Should you need to buy something that costs more than what you earn or the allowance gifted by the person who takes care of you, plan a way to pay for it in full in the shortest time possible. Then, stick to the payment plan until the whole debt is cleared. You will earn the seller's respect and make yourself a friend.

Do not wait until you have to change routes, phone numbers and friends in an attempt to escape anyone you owe. Somehow, they will find you and may make your life miserable. It is the shortest path to anxiety.

While in this neighbourhood, avoid planning with someone else's money in mind. If there is no agreement binding the person to letting you access that money, planning around it will stress you. This happens when they refuse to foot the bill after you have enjoyed the service and you are required to pay for it.

The situation gets even worse if you cannot pay in kind or that reversing the transaction requires you to downgrade to a life you have long graduated from or rejected.

How will you make more money?

The surest way to increase your income, whether earned or gifted is by investing a part of it in a way that will rake in more for you.

This differs from the general assumption that there is more money where the first amount came from. This thought persuades you to believe that you can squander what you have as the next amount makes its way towards you.

During my recovery, I realized that there are no such guarantees as far as money is concerned. Every bit of handling money must be deliberate, from the process of receiving to the actual spending. This is where saving comes in.

Whether you earn the money from a service you offer or are gifted, put aside a percentage of the sum for the purpose of handling any unforeseen situations like illnesses and furthering yourself in future. Then look for an investment vehicle that will help multiply the savings.

I have learned that even by saving as little as ten percent of any amount of money received, you can fulfil that huge desire you crave for. And this time, with pride. Or shall I say in the most legal and upright manner?

If you are investment-shy, start by opening a savings account with a bank near you and target earning interest from your savings. But you must form a habit of religiously saving a portion of any amount of money you receive. Some banks pay interest twice a year rewarding your savings efforts even more.

Then purpose in your mind what to do with the money you save. This helps to tame the temptation of withdrawing that money before the stipulated time. So think of your savings as a seedling that needs time to grow into a full tree before you eat of its fruits.

Do you find saving money impossible?

Consider the case of Lisa Nichols, the American businesswoman and motivational speaker whose savings account surprised her with $62,500. There was no magic involved. She deliberately toned down her lifestyle for three years, spending only on the basics enabling her to save 5% of every income she received from her day job.

When you master your money, you guarantee your financial wellbeing and save yourself unnecessary stress. It is that simple.

Pick Your Brain

Ordering Your Money	
How do you access money, and how much do you get in a month?	
How much money do you spend every month?	
How much money do you desire to have in your bank account by the end of next one year and why?	
Are there expenses you have incurred in the last three months that could hold you back from being where you want to be financially? *List them.*	

Do you have any debts at the moment? *If yes, list them and indicate how you intend to repay each.*	
How much do you save in a month? *If you do not, state the percentage you intend to save from this point on and start with the next income.*	

Chapter 11

How Do You Keep Your Brain Sharp?

Keeping your brain sharp through continuous learning and challenging it to figure out new ways of tackling problems around you keeps you intellectually well. This is a great way to nurture mental wellness.

This may not feel right when you are worn out, anxious or depressed. But it works wonders when turned into a habit when you are in your regular state.

The quickest way to build your intellectual wellness is through reading. Read content that helps you advance in person. Consider studying content on how to manage your finances, stay physically healthy and care for your mental health. This self-care kit is a good place to start.

Such content also builds your conversations so you have knowledge needed to help other people and contribute better in your community.

You can gather such content from your local library in form of books or you could join a book club and exchange books with likeminded people. Make sure to note down any powerful nuggets that you can apply in various parts of your life and practice them. Then, teach such to others. That way, what you learn sticks.

Consider acquiring new skills by taking free and premium courses online. You could learn how to prepare nutritious meals by watching YouTube videos of well-known healthy food lovers like Sweet Potato Soul or Fit Men Cook. Or go to Udemy.com and take a free course in an area you have always craved to. Then, wait for Black Friday season to buy the premium version of the course for about a tenth of its original price.

You could also enrol in a college or university near you for a preferred course if you prefer physical contact with your trainer. Whatever skill you settle for, ensure you have a good reason why you need it since it will cost you time, money or both in the process. That will help you stay committed should difficult times show up.

Another way of sharpening your brain is through learning a new language or how to play an instrument. The new language expands the circle of people you can communicate with, while learning how to play an instrument can be a great way of relaxing or serving people around you. And both make you look smarter, raising your self-esteem!

Then there is a fun side in nourishing your intellectual being. It involves playing brain games. You could download brain game mobile applications such as Elevate, CogniFit and Lumosity and play on your own.

But if you want to keep off gadgets while sharpening your brain, consider solving crosswords from newspapers or playing board games such as scrabble, chess or monopoly with friends.

Board games challenge you to seek ways to win against your friends, help you unwind and have an occasional laugh knocking off any stress accumulated during the day. Consider sliding in a session of board games during your book club meetups. The last thirty minutes of each session will do just fine.

Finally, you can also build your intellectual wellness by keeping a daily journal. You do not have to be a writer to journal, take it as a simple self-reflective activity to help you review your day and see how you performed.

As your review your day's journal, you will be able to identify areas where you need improvement, plan for adjustments or seek help where you need to.

When I recovered from depression and anxiety, returning to school to continue with my degree helped me train my brain to focus. It was not easy, but I had something to look forward to everyday despite the heartbreak.

I also read a variety of books and journal daily for my personal development and transformation despite completing my studies.

Pick Your Brain

Building the Brain Muscle	
What skills have you been craving to acquire but have not done much about? *List them and prepare a plan on how to start acquiring them.*	
Between playing an instrument and learning a new language, which one would you commit to pursue starting now? Why?	

Is there a board game club or book club near you? *If there is one, ask to join. If none, create one and list the kind of games and books you want to introduce in the club.*	
Plan to read one book every month for your personal development. *List the first five books you will read in the next five months here. Then, journal your progress in reading and the new habits you are forming as a result.*	

Chapter 12

Would You Help Someone Else?

There comes a time when your mental health does not revolve around you. That begins with the realization that for you to attain mental wellbeing, you have to pour out into other people's lives. This time you do it for the other person's benefit, not yours.

That is where your social wellness begins.

While having a strong support system you can go to for emotional support is required for your mental wellbeing, you too ought to reach out to others. Make it a habit to help them whenever they are in need and in the best way you can.

There are two easy ways to make this work.

Social Balancing

Start by reaching out to friends and family, and deliberately asking how they are doing. Then listen with interest.

You may not always be in a position to help, but that kind act of listening helps to ease their burdens. Think of it as a way of investing yourself socially in the lives of those around you. You will be surprised when you find yourself on the need-side of the desk; the people you invested yourself in are the same who will come to your rescue.

No matter how evil we think the world is, we are surrounded by good people. And when we initiate goodness, it boomerangs back to us. This is the other reason why I began Coffee with Queentah hangouts. I wanted to be a big sister to someone after realizing that those who rescued me from the suicide attempt were good people.

By noticing me while I leaned on the rails of Nyali Bridge, initiating a conversation and listening to me, they sowed and watered the seed of listening in me. Then during my recovery, the listening seed was nurtured so I could serve other people with its fruits.

So during the hangouts I intentionally initiate the conversations allowing my audience to uncork their bottles and let out their emotional burdens. Then they too experience the balance.

Some of the hangouts' attendees become great friends and we keep in touch long after each meet-up.

Grow Your Social Network

Nurturing your social wellbeing also demands that you expand your social network through volunteering and participating in community events on a regular basis. That way, you create means through which others can access you.

This is where Girls for Girls Africa Mental Health Foundation comes in. Besides running psychotherapy programs, I engage in projects such as distribution of free sanitary pads to communities in need. These are not hit-and-run events; they are ways to knit close relationships with people who need my assistance.

Consider having weekly meetups where you can reach out to individuals and groups in order to build strong relationships. Make an effort to connect with a new person every week and get to know them as much as they are willing to open up. Then if there is something you can do for them, do it. Otherwise stay in touch and help them get to know you better.

Avoid creating social networks for the sake of it. I have seen this habit this in the so-called networking events where someone rushes from one person to another in an attempt to get their business card and hand their own out. Such people do not bother building connections and may not even remember the people they met by name if they met them again. That is not the way to nurture social wellness. It instead makes the person look needy and repulsive.

The idea behind meeting one new person every week is to create a deliberate connection. A symbiotic relationship.

Take the social wellness a pitch higher by connecting with people far away from you. These could be people you meet on social media, like your Facebook or Instagram followers. Show them that you care by responding to their comments with niceness.

Out of a mob of fans, there is always a handful you can link up with and keep close.

You could also use technology to connect with people you went to school with a long time ago. Create or revive the friendship through sending snail mail and postcards for seasonal greetings. This may sound old school but it keeps a smile on your face and theirs as you reminisce over things that happened then. You can even venture on activities where you have common ground or support common causes.

In essence, have a social life while you still live!

Social Wellness Rules

There are a few things to watch out for while nurturing your social wellbeing; the binding matter. They include keeping love affairs, gossip and substance abuse out of it. Such habits weaken the relationships and turn budding friendship into a mess.

Instead, build the relationships on the foundation of kindness, truthfulness and pure love for fellow mankind. This way, when anyone in your network is in need, they will feel free to speak out.

The greatest commandment in nourishing your social wellness is this, 'do unto others as you would have them do unto you'.

Pick Your Brain

Dare to Nurture Your Social Wellbeing	
Former schoolmates' hunt *List 20 former schoolmates you would like to get in touch with and make an effort to look for each one of them both online and offline.* *Then take the hunt further by establishing a relationship with them.*	
List three community events taking place around you and seek to be part of them. *While there, find out ways to volunteer with them and get to know the participants in depth. State here the service you will offer to the groups organizing those community events.*	

In every meetup you attend, make a habit of listening to and noticing the good things about the each one of the participants and compliment them about such. *Note such good things here after the event.*	
List the kind of activities you can do with different people you meet during the community events you attend to strengthen the relationships.	

Chapter 13

Do You Care For the Hood?

You should, because the environment you live in reciprocates the love you give to it dictating your mental health state.

Being human means it is up to you to take care of your personal surroundings, whether natural or that which you have created. The easiest way to see the effect your habitat has on mental wellness is by comparing a dumping site to the posh estates in your surroundings.

How would you describe the state of the people living at a dumpsite?

Consider their happiness, ability to solve everyday problems, general physical health and their lifespan.

Do you think they differ from those who live in the well-organized estates where access to food, medical assistance and recreational facilities is possible?

Now look around your home and workplace. How easy is it to access items that you need in short notice?

This is where orderliness comes in. You would not want to get exasperated over looking for a pen at your work desk, knife in your kitchen or a free chair to sit in when you get home, would you?

When your surroundings are clean and organized, you are at peace. You feel in control and are able to respond to different needs fast.

The same goes for the outer surrounding. Your brain is at a ready state when you are in a calm environment. Like while walking along the beach, in a park with water fountains or flowers, or a neighbourhood you consider safe.

Note, you are always bothered by things that concern you or require your input first. So if you can see the mess, you can do something about it.

Part of your call now is to make your environment your business and demand from it only what you have given to it. Make it worthy of your living, and in return, you will be at peace. That is a huge part of your mental wellbeing!

Pick Your Brain

Making Your World a Better Place	
Start with your home; would you consider it clutter free? *List a number of adjustments you are willing to make starting now so that when you walk in, it embraces you with peace.*	List the adjustments starting with those that will not cost much if at all.
A peaceful workplace *Regardless of where you work, is there anything you can add or remove to make your operation less of a headache?*	List the adjustments to make starting with those that require less authorization and are affordable.

A beautiful neighbourhood *Are there activities that take place occasionally to care for the environment that you can participate in?*	List the activities. If none, note the areas of need and begin rooting for changes in such. Your environment is your business.
A Wonderful World *What causes can you join for the betterment of other people around the world?*	List causes you can join and support now. They do not have to affect you directly.

Part 4

Go Rock The World!

Chapter 14

You Are Free

Congratulations for coming this far!

Not only have you been deliberate about nourishing your mental health, but also your holistic wellness. This means you have set yourself free from opportunistic circumstances that would compromise your overall health. And now you are free to assist other people to do likewise.

That is how I feel every time I meet up with various groups when conducting Yoga and various other meetups. I feel free. I feel gifted to give to others. I feel ready to conquer the world.

That does not mean I do not come across tough times, I do. But I have learned to reach out for help and to help. I am glad that I went through the tough times earlier in my life; they prepared me for a life with many other people. Now I know better to be nice to myself and to others. To be kind to myself and others. And to love myself and in the process love others. To love you.

It is the reason this self-care kit exists. It is my way of saying, 'I love you and I want the best for you, just as I want the best for me.'

You too are free to be nice, to be kind and to love.

Pick Your Brain

The affirmations below are borrowed from thekindmindclub.com. I use them in different circumstances in my life. You can too.

Affirmations For Your Mental Wellness	
Begin your day with these affirmations	I have the power to create the life I want. I have the power to control my thoughts. I am confident I can achieve every goal I set. I am at peace with my past. I love and embrace my flaws. I choose to be happy right now. I deserve the best. I am open and comfortable with the unknown. I am resilient, strong, and brave. I am letting go of all that no longer serves me.

When you feel less inclined to forgive yourself for something you did in the past, note it down in a separate piece of paper and declare these affirmations. *When you are through, destroy the paper, with confidence.*	I am human. I acted in the best way I was capable of in that moment. I am a grown person. I am grateful for increased insight, and the opportunity to make better choices from now on. I accept this about myself, I allow myself to be at peace with this. I forgive myself. I am worthy of love, acceptance and happiness. Any sadness I may feel is only temporary and I will overcome it. I have so much to offer this world. Everything will be ok.

Use these affirmations when you need emotional healing. *When you are hurting, write your immediate feelings in a piece of paper and declare these affirmations. Then destroy that piece of paper, with confidence.*	Today is a new day. I trust that my faith in the universe will gift me with all that I need in life; I am in the healing process and getting better day by day. I am stronger than I may realize. I take things step by step and do not put the pressure on myself to do more than I can handle. I release all past trauma and pain. I replace it with pure love and forgiveness. When things start to worry me, I take a deep breath and release the fear. I am safe. I focus on the good in my life.

Then show yourself some love because you deserve it! *Create a small card with the words, 'I love me' on one side and 'I love you' on the other side. Make it colourful, print and laminate it and keep it in a place you can see it often.*	I love me. I am worth loving. I choose to stop apologizing for being me. I release negative self-talk. I love the person I am becoming. I am proud of where I am at. I believe in myself and my abilities. I am radiant and I accept myself unconditionally. I am whole.

For Your Abundant Wellness

This is not the end; it is the beginning of your holistic transformation, a good reason why you should return to the beginning of this kit and read through the responses you gave in every worksheet. Print them out, attach them to your journal and review them on a weekly basis.

Mental wellness, as you now know is an everyday affair. So use the worksheets, your initial responses and your journal to help you keep a tab on it. Then at the end of every month, compare your previous responses to your new status.

Let's Keep in Touch

Twitter: @AuthorQueentah

Instagram: @officialqueentahwambulwa

Stay Well!